evening primroses

—

Gabby Loomis-Amrhein

Copyright © 2021 Gabby Loomis-Amrhein.

1st Edition.

All rights reserved. No part of this book may be reproduced in any form or by any electronic or mechanical means, including information storage and retrieval systems, without prior permission in writing from the publisher, except for brief quotations embodied in critical articles and reviews. For more information, contact Recenter Press, recenterpress@gmail.com.

evening primroses by Gabby Loomis-Amrhein
ISBN: 9798717392037

Written by Gabby Loomis-Amrhein.
Editing and cover design by Terra Oliveira.

Versions of the following poems appear in the following publications:
borrow pits — Hematopoiesis Press.
view from the bald — Hoxie Gorge Review.
libraries and *nectar and meteorites* — Sheepshead Review.
cornfield forts and *32DD $1.99* — Recenter Press Poetry Journal.

Published in April 2021 by Recenter Press.

Instagram: @birdingwhilequeer
www.recenterpress.com

*for the birds,
truly.*

PREFACE

—

Each summer when I was young, my mother planted evening primroses in her garden on the side of the dead end, country road where we lived. Evening primroses bloom, as their name suggests, in the evening, and their bloom happens in such a way that they actually burst open in a matter of seconds. Many evenings, we'd go out to watch together, and often a handful of neighbors came over to join, sometimes with food and drink. Years later I came out as a gardener, then as trans, then as a farmer and naturalist. Evening primroses are queer, even among flowers. They are crepuscular, existing in the spaces between night and day, growing in the bed on the edge of the road, flourishing in the margins, despite the margins, maybe helping to heal in the margins.

I wear overalls while using a machete and a scythe, and skirts while walking the woods after work. I feel a kinship with deer, the dawn chorus of passerines, the language in the patterns of bark. "The country" in the so-called united states is not often thought to be a particularly welcoming place for queer people. Regardless of the levels of truth in this sentiment for each of us, I'd like these poems to complicate the idea that the country is not queer itself, that our presence in it inevitably leads to queer exodus to the city, and that in the edge, the margins, there can be no belonging or home. I did not write or collect these poems to deny the trauma and struggle of living a rural life as a queer person, in fact, many of them were borne of such experiences. I write these poems to remind myself, to remind other country queers, the queer spaces in the city, the queer mist on the edge of the queer wood, that despite the margins, we belong in the world.

crepuscular

everything is trans at the edge of everything else,
growing like grandmother's morning glories
out of the whiskey barrel, up the rail
curling 'round the mailbox
where the postal worker who hates fags
gently places love letters from you to me and vice versa
real queer woman to real queer person,
with hearts beating like fireflies across hayfields,
both of which are trans
in their fallowness, and the infallibility of their luminescence,
in their light i sit
among the h/edges of all things.

i have a total crush on spring

you can tell by february
that spring will come back because the smell of skunks will start blooming
it is the most enchanting fragrance you can imagine
their sometimes-bodies dotting the roadside like bee stings

winter aconite will shoot up so prolifically
you'd think the blooms are counting
the number of trans people murdered so far this year
and you'll cry for the nature of your growing anomalousness

you have lived here long enough that you can tell if it will be cooler or warmer
than yesterday by looking at which direction the mourning doves are facing
on the telephone wires
you have lived here long enough to know when men place severed mourning dove wings
in envelopes and send them off for verification of death

remembrance is a mercurial season that sits beneath all others
as vernal as the tadpoles in the stream
and as pernicious as the snapper beaks and raccoon paws
that snatch them into the darkness of their bellies

but in spring, memories become subsumed
inside the first afternoon of rolling a joint under maple buds
and sunning your bare feet on the warm roof

hoar frost sundays

clammy feet
between warm thighs

        what remains of wood thrush eggshell
          tucked inside an envelope

                        nakedness
                  in a large borrowed bed

borrow pits

from mid-november to roughly the beginning of april two things happen:
one: teal and wigeons, snow geese, buffleheads, tundra swans, mergansers, canvasbacks,
thousands and *thousands* and *thousands* of ducks and geese stop over
in the borrow pits of the limestone mines of this county.
two: my heart breaks, over and over, every year.
i say that first to convey how it feels each time,
but really it is more like my heart is shedding skin like a snake,
a metaphor, but a real metamorphosis.
entering into a process of self-care that leaves oneself deadly-vulnerable,
coming out the other side soft and new and tender,
only to realize it is a process that is not over.

i grew up not thinking twice about borrow pits,
other than wondering at age six about their turquoise hue
and realizing at age fifteen that they are unsafe to swim in
even compared to the creek that flows into the woods from the cow pasture.
now i know that *borrow* is a misnomer,
because nobody asked if they could take anything,
and they certainly aren't giving it back.
and worse, the people who make them
usually just walk away,
leaving the earth to scar,
throwing trash into the pits in their wake.

borrow pits are wounds,
infected, scarring, but mostly loss.
they are holes,
and what is left after something is stolen.

winter birds, however, are like hope inside them.
they are the good bacteria,
softly whinnying and alighting on the water at dusk
to turn scar into story,
the sunset into a corner, turned.

i scuff my shoe on the stones at the top of the crater rim

and my heart on the hope of some kind of spring,
and notice a snakeskin at my feet.
this place has been a home for thousands of birds during hard months,
and maybe the old self someone left at my toes will serve to help build the nest of another.
the edge of the wound at which i stand,
no longer seems to contain the entire horizon,
and at this moment the sunset expands,
and i can feel myself breathe deep for the first time since october.

salamander gay

i did not know i was a salamander gay
until i walked into the woods at night
i felt like a miner with my headlamp
foraging unseeingly about in the detritus
so gingerly and bare-handed
my body curled fetal in the warm breath
of the first weird february starlight
caught against the collarbone of an abandoned quarry
spring still seeping just perfect
and full of one whole jelly-dog
cradled in my palms
telling of the silent moonlight parade to come

instagram poetry book tours of the future pt. a

what percentage of the profits do we get?
what percentage of the profits are our bodies?
is it still profitable to be trans?
how can i describe the difference between profit
and just wanting healthcare and shelter
how much are our life expectancies shortened?
when did they get sick?
when did they die?
when will i get sick?
what if we all helped each other?
what if everything here wasn't stolen from someone
who stole it from someone?
how hard are our hearts beating in relation to our profitability?
our tactically enforced brevity?
each other?
how often do you need me to wear a dress for you to believe i'm a woman?
how often do i need to wear a dress for you to believe that i am a woman
        enough for me to believe that i am a woman?
will you like my free posts? will you buy my book?
will you post it in your instagram story with the "yass" graphic?
do you know where that word comes from?
whose mouths are silent because?
will you "love it" after reading 3 poems and not pick it up again?
will you love the aesthetic of the dust it collects on your shelf more
and how it will elucidate to your friends how eruditely allyish you were
before it was cool?

valentine

wool sweaters
nettle beer
warm fires.

winter kisses.

the water sitting in the dimple
at the bottom of the colander
after everything.

chickens in the bathtub

the day before the state barred gatherings and non-essential work
i brought home a short dozen plymouth rock chicks
and we bestowed the comfort of our bathtub
upon the saintly presence of hungry beaks

huddled together under the rose sunset
we and an uncountable people globally wrote an exquisite corpse
togetherness in being alone
food, shelter, love
mostly solidarity

by the warm glow from the grow light we watched
the wizards and the mathematicians
mapping the future of the wave over our bodies
and we began to learn again
how to hold each other's breath
and how to hold each other's dreams

crackling

delighted shrieks splitting clam spines and snail shells,
gibbous waxing moons calcifying in mounds beside
hulls and berries, middens of seed and shit on waterlogged drift
rising above the current, a sundial beneath the stars,
casting shadows into the river depths,
hiding silver fish from feasting paws and gnashing teeth,
crackling echoes of springtime raccoon gatherings
hugging the riparian, reminding of the everywhereness of home

pisces day

are our barnred bodies only of utility?
the mosses and lichen will make their way through the knots in our siding/
the flutter of our hearts.
what we make of the rust is only a translation of decay
which is only a translation of what it means to be.
the mortised summer beams
and tenoned whale rib joists cradling the floor
can only hold for another hundred years
of dancing and threshing and loss
before, as an homage to the old ordovician seabed on which it sits,
shall necessarily melt back into the silt.
the rust of our tools will freckle about our feet among the jewelweed
the wooden flesh of our gay forearms and thighs
letting out a decompositional sigh of relief
for being made of prolonged dust and aridity
at the bottom of an ocean of midwestern sky
the angle of planetary repose cutting through time
the only definitive step for the pace of a thought
and those it proposes to possess
is to die,
and move on,
as we were meant to
around the circle of becoming
part of this stone again.

doctor farmer doula carpenter

when people started getting sick
not january sick but
the waves that came around my birthday sick
the waves containing the tugboat of spring equinox
when hospitals in new york city said
help us

when the feds sent aid to queens
to stem the curve
the undulating waves
in lieu of ventilators—refrigerated trucks
collecting bodies like grain
the police state has a knack for suffocating people
especially in new york it seems
especially those who tend plants it seems
especially those who cross borders it seems
just to do work to feed people
just to make money to send home to feed people
just to feed people

my friend is a doctor
my friend is a farmer
my friend is a doula
my friend is a carpenter

all the roughness of their hands
can be mapped conversely
onto the tender space they hold in the world

from the field to the truck
to the bakery to the truck
to the house to the mouth
to the soul to the hospital
and unto the truck we shall return

the genera of a dresser top

13-	¾" screws for hoophouse lath
1-	muskrat tooth found in creek
4-	receipts
1-	poetry collection
1-	large sex toy
1-	2oz jar of homemade calendula cream
2-	u.s. quarters
7-	house plants
x-	dust motes
1-	bra
3-	field guides
1-	u.s. penny
3-	small sex toys
4-	2.5" screws for chicken coop perches
1-	novel
1-	u.s. nickel
2-	gaffs
2-	dried clovers
2-	half drunk cups of tea
27-	seed packets of radish, arugula, kale
3-	u.s. dimes
2-	pens
1-	pair of binoculars
1-	brilliant spot where the sunrise pops in to say hello

bottle rockets

during the minute between
7:19 p.m. and 7:20 p.m.
on april 3rd, 2015,
159 people said "i love you"
through 8 sets of telephone wires
along fairfield road
glowing brilliant orange-on-fire,
reflecting the sunset.

for april

in a month cut an orange in half
nail it to a tree open face out
little wending suns will flit about
singing songs called
syrup
lemon
hope

porchlight love///missouri primroses

small poems laugh like sips of springwater
and your fingertips whirl around mine like bicycle rides in summertime

i want to be with you while our laugh lines grow deep
and we can drink tea in the spring,
our bare feet smiling on the worn wood of a front porch

and even if the seasons get out of order
we can rewrite where we are into words like honey and incandescent and

the last thing i want to tell you right now is this—
i'm more glad than i ever thought a person could be
that the poem which began with you leaving me nearly speechless
by the compost pile six octobers ago with your cumulonimbus laugh,
has unfurled with love, bursting like missouri primroses
into the way we hold each other at night.

ally ©

everyone is "rad" on instagram or one-on-one
until their friend walks up and won't use my pronouns
and they sit with their hands in their laps and turn red
filling up with the words they won't say

everyone is "rad" around other allies©
until i come over and can't drink beer with this t-blocker
and everyone gets quiet and never offers to get another option
next time, or next time, or next time

everyone is "rad" and loud about the latest article they read
about trans people being murdered
have you heard? about trans people being murdered
isn't it so tragic? about trans people being murdered

trans people being murdered
ringing in my ears

everyone is "rad" on their eggshells
silent like moths trying not to fuck up
fucking up inherently fucking up intimacy or just compassion
i did not come out to you for this distance

migratory restlessness

every single person on earth
looks great in a dress
i want you to know that
i wanted you to know that

there's a way all midwestern kids
try to escape their bodies
the heat the money the dust

driving in rectangles
whether in seance exorcism or exaltation
our maps get messy
and tumble into moments of falling apart

i hit a robin up there once
cresting the glacial gastroliths
along the county line
wasn't able to grieve them til now either

i didn't swerve and you did
i don't know what that means
i don't know if i want it to mean

there is something about fire here
the eternal ginger of the robins breast
the month of may

i miss getting to know you
i miss you getting to know you

but i suppose you've found a way to do that still
probably by a lake in the low light
you finally have this humidity beat
nestled in for nightfall
and tomorrow
learning a new kind of flight

may 11th

i am a poem i wouldn't show my mother
not in the sense that i am undeserving of her love
or that i do not receive it as i am
but in an i-am-my-own-mother-too sort of way
having had to mother myself through crushing on men
when i still thought i was one
to being worthy of my own love as a woman no one sees

as i am
a turn of phrase i have barely potty trained

a turn of phrase who i hope will help me with the farm chores
when she is strong enough

a turn of phrase who one day will tell me what she really means
in a day late mothers day poem

i happen to like my tea a little cooler

than you
and so i sit with my hands wrapped around this baked earth
i feel yours mending it into a sensation of home
in the pre-dawn light
in a tree frog chorus
among fireflies across the dewing wheat
in my body
and in yours

a field guide for surviving dysphoria pg. 63

sometimes until top surgery
you can walk out into a hay field
and leave your clothes
way out in the middle of june
you can feel the moonheat on your butt
you can close your eyes
fireflies swirling around your knees
do you feel the slightest breeze
it is the world
you are gorgeous

preconceived notions of transness and rest stops

a gas station in southwest ohio is a point in space.
at night it is an incandescence that attracts moths and birds,
often to their death.

the highway is a ribbon of light
on which i never want to stop gliding,
and from which i always want to leave,
and beside which is rarely ever safe in a blouse.

my body is trans,
and my friend's body is trans.
he drove a semi truck as long as he could.

i needed gas coming back from the city.
dressing how i wished for pride put me there.
"i should have gotten gas before"
"i should not have come"
"i should put my work coat on to step out of my car"

i wonder how much longing/confusion/understanding
pools in staring eyes
as often as i wonder how much violence has collected there.
have you ever stared back?
have you ever said "what"
have you ever wondered if you accidentally killed yourself
with a bigot's body in frustration?

what is the body here,
stuck, briefly,
fluttering upon a buzzing node,
waiting to wade back into a ribbon of light,

and out of sight,
a flutter.

sweet pea

i think of you often
non-nodulated and late-flowering

my sweet pea
fabulous fabeaceous fag of the fields
men have so much concern and worry for the nakedness of your roots
for the spines you grew to keep pleistocene megafauna at bay
how they puncture the tires of their precious tractors
how can they till the nursery you tend
with thorns in their feet
how can they compact and corn and soy and combine with your incessant mattering
aerating and blowing away and exhausting when you are just exhausting them
my queen
i look to you so for guidance
your copse is sacred
your pinnate fingers gingerly cradle warblers
ushering them over and again into flight
your toes dipped forever in the complicated water where i also grew
i know what it means to be a river queen
field-edge and flowering
and i learned it from you

family pt. ii

light
from june
and from fireflies
fills my stomach when
we roll onto our sides in bed
and make the shape of a pear
between us, the size of a purr
the chatter of titmice
breaking against
the glass of
our
bedroom
windowpanes
trickles away into
fading starlight
your morning
eyes
meet mine
in a world
of hums

scissor-tailed flycatchers///missouri, midsummer

i wish i could tell you what it means to be your big sister.
i've been trying to write it down for weeks now—
every time i try i think of when you came to visit me in st. louis.
we drove all the way out to darst bottom road,
with the river and the sacred shade under those massive trees,
across fields unbroken as far as the eye could see,
in the middle of nowhere, missouri
just because i wanted to show you scissor-tailed flycatchers;
how elegant they are with their
bonewhite bodies
peachpit bellies
blood-red underwings
and most of all their swirling dresses, those tails in flight!
you knew i also needed to get away from the noise and rush,
the heat from such tremendous concrete and asphalt
i'll never not be a country queer at heart
i don't even remember if we saw birds or not
only taking turns at the wheel of that old, white car—
the same one that almost killed us on that mountain in west virginia—
driving the whole length of the single, gravel lane of darst bottom,
each in turn sitting out the side of the passenger window
feeling the wind washing away the dust, stifling humidity, endsmeet, everything,
missouri, midsummer,
washed away in the hot wind and the sun.

race yourself home
    (for Sam)

squinting against july down wilberforce road
spiteful camouflage with the word reckless
mapped onto us by the old gays living off our rent checks

coasting downhill
eyes closing every three seconds for one second
matching the pace of the dotted yellow line

country chicory blurring towards us
washing over our shoulders
constellations of wildflowers
like the ones you gave
spilling over the lip of a jar
little stars of queer joy
celestial reminders brushing the sandled ankles
of everything zooming past
i see you and the world is better for a moment

32DD $1.99

the cheapest boobs i found that didn't come out of a dumpster or free box
were at a st. vincent thrift store in ohio.
you never left my side and the maga hats and camo pants
walked on by

when the elderly woman shopping for underwear came up behind me
you nonchalantly held up the first négligée
that connected with your left hand on the rack

"how about this one?"

i wonder how many times those words
from the mouths of loving partners and friends
kept people walking
let trans sisters buy the padded thrift store tits
they'd been longing to have for months
removed a slap or a bruise from the future
saved a life

ordovichia

a bit ago
before people
the midwest was a seabed

fossil evidence is unearthed
and often obscured in cornstubble grazing
razing silty shoals to feed ungulates to feed humans

but listen

on a breath-held humid august night
when nothing moves
the dangling stoplight angler fish
will bear witness

to the thought of a breeze
then to the stillness

and unto the ocean
for a moment
everything returns

Arnold's pool

when i was gay
you had a crush on me
we both wore short shorts
i was turning compost
you grinned wider than the august sky
held between the tines of a hay fork

when we are gay
you work for an older writer
he keeps stories and notes and love
and needs help letting go
his garden is overgrown and perfect
the skylights inside illuminate motes of acceptance
and of not yet please

a moment
it is july
it is afternoon
i am drenched on the farm
you are drowning in papers
Arnold leaves the house
you call me to say
there is a pool out back. come over.
the gayest shit i have ever heard
we strip inside the gates behind the jungle
you jump in and i see the entire night sky
i jump into the only pool i may have ever felt safe in

we leave as quickly as we came
field mice gleaning grain
hiding out in the edge before the great haying
til the night comes again

view from the bald

from up on the bald the trail ahead is a series of fading, chopped-up curves,
like hair on the kitchen floor, cut in rage and frustration and heartache,
and like a good backpacking trip, there is the immediate regret of letting the moments fall away.

i want to tell you it is a funny thing to go bald
        just not on the days when i look in the mirror, perplexed,
and remember that to most *i am a wrong thing*, to other queers, even other trans women.
i want to tell you that balding is a funny thing,
        but more often it is sadness, and rarely,
glimpses of beauty.

hiking among brush and grasses, without a tree around,
        my gaze tumbles down the slope, across the creek, and up the other side,
several mountains over, fading into the sky.
every peak around is stark and treeless, bald and beautiful,
        mountains among mountains, with the best views in the entire range.

here are some water facts:

i am so dehydrated.
i only peed 3 times today and the average person who drinks enough water pees 8 times every 24 hours.

the amount of corn in ohio and other bread basket states directly contributes to the amount of humidity therein.

the only thing in ohio that sweats more than i do is corn.

clouds are mountains that sit on top of floating lakes.
i learned that when i was five years old on an airplane and i have no intention of fact-checking it.

birds exhibit bathing behavior in water, dust, sand, sunlight, and wind.

i exhibit bathing behavior twice per day in late july and early august on days that i have farm shifts.

i do not usually bathe in anything except water, though in winter i bathe in sunlight,
and when things come up i occasionally rinse with wind, dust and sand.

render me riparian

here.
my body.
render me riparian,
    under the dappled shade,
    in a golden cloud of pollen,
    projections of tulip poplars masking my face.
riffle my goosebumps,
    with babblings in almost-word-shapes like
    brood comb, fish, melt, and plop.
salamander my understanding of
    what it means to be too hot,
    and what it means to be hotter,
    what it means to be water,
    and what it means to be wet.
crawdad my scars,
    gently crawling backwards,
    away from ago, beyond the next oxbow.
tanager my feet,
    into july-tough on limestone and clam shards,
    filling spaces among maples
    with principally red sounds.

here.
my body.
render me riparian,
    compress my lungs underwater,
    cool my skin and my blood,
    run through my hair,
    until we float downstream from ourselves,
    carving this world into a canyon
    safe enough for every bee.

goat ppl

goats and people both stare at me
when i wear 'femmy' clothes
you know—
the ones with frills, or lace, or straps

goats try to bite
and sometimes when people don't
i wish they would

cornfield forts

what does it mean to reflect on a tomboy girlhood as a trans woman?

climbing down the limestone cliffs with friends
to jump topless into the swimming hole,
drying in the dappled sunlight on the bank,
picking mulberries and catching crawdads,
feasting 'round makeshift firepits,
tang of honeysuckle and osage,
owls caterwauling as the sky turns rose,
distant storm clouds a burnt orange.

first drink of whiskey sitting on the back of a rusted allis-chalmers,
barn door wide open to smell the rain,
three pairs of hands flicking pebbles
into the water-worn groove from the tin roof overhang,
humming with the buzz of rain and of spirits in our bellies,
laughing like the rustle of mice in the timothy and clover overhead,
finally falling asleep as the clouds part ways like a sigh,
our bodies wrapped in flannel, washed in moonlight.

sneaking out into fulton's cornfield in late august,
half a fifth of bulleit and a handful of pocket-knives,
cutting stalks from the middle of the field in a ten-by-ten square,
weaving them along the edge of standing corn,
a giant basket, surrounded by the smells of summer with a pang of sadness;
the stars above and the soil below, knowing this was already over.

nectar and meteorites

i bought two tickets
north out of the city
/
looking up as i walked
grand central station slowed to mosquitoes
humming in a sappy pre-amber memory
/
all the way out
in the middle of the floor i stopped
carved into the bedrock of manhattan
and as i stood under pisces
you came to me out of nowhere
with fresh peaches to share
/
the footprints we left
became a constellation
with so many stars
it will take us forever and a telescope
to recount them

Pinus dysphoriensis

pining for a time i'm not sure i've had
    yet always have,

staring across a lake at dusk,
sun-dry skin,
hair-raised against a cooling breeze.

flying out on a rope swing
far enough to startle the loons,
rippling to the stars.

pawpaw custard pie

there is a thrift store platter
on which we alternately keep our cherished things
fruit, house plants, baked goods

it has a body made of red clay
which many adults say is not safe
you look down
knowing much about clay
and how bodies are deemed safe or not

this plate contains a grey sort of sky that also holds sunshine
enough so that tangerine and marmalade bloom inside of it
bluets and chicory too

this wonderful dish entered our home through your hands
and a pie baking contest
it was september
i was several years in love with you
in a fruit bringing way
and in southern ohio that means the lifting of sweat
the descent of morning fog
the softening of pawpaws

you read as you do and read more as you do
you hmmmed
there was magic in a book
both arcane and survivance
which you tried on the crowd
community day as they called it
and my god did we eat
the plate was the contest winning prize
and our bellies were the winning rounds
and the pawpaw seeds the winning coins
rounded in turn in pockets and worn to scarify and drop
through compost and time into humid fruition again

chicken of the woods

in the period just following summer
and i don't mean early energetic booty shorts summer
i mean wring out your work shirt sweating summer
there are two things to look forward to

there is the rope swing into the creek in the shade of the day
and there is the growth of brilliant orange gems in the pitch of the night
the night which, after two months of unrelenting, 3am, wet stillness
cools

and there is a breeze

autumn has been invited to return on its haunches
and fanning the royal colors into fruition beyond ripeness
into decay
sulphur shelves
blooming, in a way
lighting up the dry trunks of dead ash and oak
lanterns in the forest at dusk
lighting the way to a skillet
a simple country meal
a royal country feast

how many urinary tract infections

are incurred annually by women afraid to piss
in public bathrooms for fear of men seeing them
or rather, for fear of them failing to

rural kroger bathrooms
usually perfectly uneventful
sometimes just so happen to align like inconvenient stars

3 cis men and 1 tranny.
i always pee before going to the grocery now

my consolation is in their nature
3 shitty cis men in a rural kroger bathroom
their mark in history
a stain in a fading memory
crumpled in a parking lot trash bin
less significant than every discarded coke can

libraries

we worked for endsmeet and vegetables under the sun
got our new, irregular moles burned off
cried and screamed and raged when our loved ones
        were taken from us
we burned and we sweated until we soaked
        ran harefooted to slaughter the hens
when the foxes would not finish the job
we washed our hands of the blood and buried them
        to lay daffodils for the rest of their lives
we turned our beds of noxious weeds and nasty men
        and we ordered pizza after shift once and drank wine

gardeners are simultaneously the roughest and most tender people
        our hands; libraries of scars and calluses,
        removing seeds from gossamer envelopes
cradling them into the soil
        encouraging them up into the light
        to bear the best fruits of their volition
and we grew that way and held each other
        against the roughest weathering,
into the most fruitful summers of our days.

would have been named

biting into a late september plum
letting the juice pool in my palm
drip down my wrist

        starlings in the walls
        fox squirrels in the attic
        wild garlic since quarantine started

                lit by the dark of the new moon
                we let our honey on the wild ginger
                flowering about the forest floor

        windows open
        tree frogs singing
        it's ok to be from a swamp

flight

i

i am going to work 14 hours a day for the next 31 days
mucking stalls and throwing bales into a loft
so i can afford to give my friend $250 to help pay for her ticket
out of the dead-end job,
the co-worker she runs from in the parking lot,
the ballfield where the boys called her faggot and
choked her until she said uncle,
the grandma who stopped giving her twenties at christmas when she found out
the dollar store clerk who tells everyone what underwear and makeup she buys
the whispers which, no matter how strong she is, get into her head
and the love we share despite it all

ii

i am going to work 14 hours a day for the next 31 days
mucking stalls and throwing bales into a loft
so my grandma still thinks i'm a man,
so i can afford underwear and makeup from the next town over,
thrift store skirts sandwiched between flannel shirts in the checkout line,
binoculars for looking at birds in my secret meadow,
and a buck knife in case the ballfield boys come around while i'm out there,
watching the goldfinch picking through thistle seed,
the blackbird as standoffish as myself and louder than i am quiet,
and looking up to the sound of a mixed flock of geese,
wind across feathers, thundering north-northwest,
carrying me as righteously as the bus did my friend into the city

iii

my back is not like it once was;
i no longer carry a hundred pounds of hay at once,
but i've also dropped my secrets,
and my load is a little lighter, though thin.
i started wearing dresses into town when my friend went missing,
and everyone shied away like deer from a clap.
the ballfield boys' children think i'm a witch,
and i play the enigma in my herb garden
and the communion i keep with feathered friends.

i flew out to visit once,
saw the new burger joint she worked,
the new friends she flocked safely with.
the call came three years later,
and i have counted every chickadee to this day
hoping she'll come back.

what kind of sunflower is your junk

the reinscription of monster onto my body by the cis gaze
sits in the center of a seesaw
and on either end the dual citadel
cumbersome and routine

but honestly,

ppl just wanna know

the dirt
the junk
my literal junk though
what do i plan to do with it
how do i like to fuck

the perennial pleasure of perineal play
(can you imagine the look on your face as you read this)

let me tell you though
realizing it is ok to feel joy in the body
is different than having access to that joy

do you want to try to understand my heartache
do you really want to know the dirt
to touch your hands to the soil for the first time
since last autumn when you put your garden to bed
not realizing all you wanted was the spring

the difference between anal and perenial
is not temporal so much as it is clima(c)tic
we are talking about zones here
and the difference between a self-seeding annual and one that is not
is a matter of care and communication and trust
which coincidentally applies to assumptions of foreverness

the problem, in the end,
with cishet sexual codices

has less to do with the fading arcanity of the patriarch
than the fact that we were never given space to ask
what kind of sunflower is my junk

heimeanshe

when a liberal
is told a tale of a tran,
they must support,
and they must do so loudly and broadly
for all to hear, especially the tran
                                  i love you
from across the street
                                  you are special
from a block down the sidewalk
                                  you are brave
alone on a trail in the woods
                                  you are not alone
in a public setting
in front of everyone
did you know he
i mean she
he i mean
she
he i
mean she
is one too
and did you know that well you are so brave and so lovely so loudly
and did you know that when you are not around
you are a hush
you are a whisper
a stutter
a retort
a question?

drop biscuits

what does it mean to be a gay farmer
smoking a joint at let off
warming yr junk in front of the stove making drop biscuits
snacking on radishes with a pad of butter
all of these things
and none of these things
the earth in your fingers
your fingers in the earth

saltmarsh

growing up i was told roughly 75% of my body is water.
growing up i was told roughly that i was a boy.

i used to have roughly 75% boy friends.
they played roughly and somewhere between when i was told it was normal to roughhouse
instead of look at plants and wear skirts
i began to enjoy boyness in a stockholm syndrome sort of way.

they played roughly with their words and their bodies, not unfriendly exactly, but quite unforgiving.
it was not all bad, and i can't blame them for what they learned, or where they learned it.
or something.

the women and girls i knew growing up had some kind of relationship with water.
it was intrinsically tied to bleeding and the moon and the stars and tides.

i have a good relationship with the moon,
though i've been told it can never be like those of the afab women i know.
i didn't recognize the jealousy i harbored from being sorted out of this relationship until i was 21.
to that point i am to this day cutting ropes and breaking cleats on the boats of internalized transmisogyny docked in the slips between my ribs.

i love big storms,
unless they're tornadoes:
the love of my life taught me that boys are a lot like tornadoes.
it doesn't rain inside them, nor do they tend to pass over saltwater.
ghosts, one might say, hauntings.

we are told in the construction of boyhood that men don't cry.
i was never given specific percentages in school,
but i think it's a safe bet that there is more water and salt
pent up inside a misgendered woman than an afab woman who has a safe space to cry,

and that when trans women cry it is like a tide no one has ever seen,
swollen from the violence of men and of sacred womanhood,
and on the nights that the moon is largest,
we are oceans of words and sentiments, incidents and prayers,
from platitudes of the love and hate given to and born inside of us,
to the most queer and ineffable corners of our shores.

gingerly

did you know that if you spend most of your life feeling
so distant from your own body
while also being caged in it
you can disappear?
we often do.

there are few ways to cross back.
most of the time it can't happen
there is a permanence that lodges as a dwarf planet
onto the outer solar system of everyone
who never noticed

when you were here
when you were not

but let me tell you
that is how i learned to come back once or twice
caring for myself
i read Bellwether
tenderly softened my fingers
taught myself where to find my yes
on either side of my no
a hmmm and a hymn

church can be feeling pleasure
when the world would have you feel none
church can be your body
under the heat of the stars

instagram poetry book tours of the future pt. b

there are publishing conventions for writing a poem about having a marginalized body.

1: turbulence.
the market is currently in the mood for being reminded that it is not the only thing suffering.
it would like to eat another poem about decolonization by a colonized author,
it would like to eat another poem about life after trans misogynist violence by a trans author.
it would like to season your disdain for it with post-colonial analysis.
how many marginalized authors can it fit on the bookshelf when no one is left?

2: listicle that shit.
list poems critical of list poems are so 2012, but this is the culture of the instructed task.
nostalgia for looking forward can be commodified,
and the semblance of assurance that one day the list will be obsolete
will be the outline on the mannequin of your body in the bookstore window,
whether or not it's a boarded up box,
whether or not you're in a boarded up box.

3: reject your laminarity.
anything that feels like mmmmmmmmmmm and hmmmmmmmmm
and soft and just
alright
just alright
for once
won't sell a book

alright just for once won't bring anyone back
who is already gone.

4: and so.
at the end of the day.

at the end of this day in the year of someone else's lord
we may write a grievance
we may write an elegy
but by my body we may write a joy
we may write a book on our terms
and throw it through the window into ourselves
in every neighborhood under the sun
every construction under the market's thumb
into everything keeping us down.

of much trouble///in an eddy, maybe

we leave each other, ultimately,
in a greater coming together
than we could ever imagine

in an eddy, maybe,
of rhizomes around the false ribs—and the true
doing the breathing for

the garnering of energy
in the cycling of life
not against the entropy of the universe
but in an eddy, maybe,
around the paddle
in the fading

and if it wouldn't be of much trouble
if you find yourself in such a situation
in which it doesn't inconvenience you—
you wouldn't mind engraving upon my stone an epitaph:
"i came up with answers but i forget them now"

take the gaff

i am shopping at target
to buy control-top pantyhose
because everyone online says
gaffs that are sold as gaffs
won't get me more bang for my buck.

i should back up:
target supports trans folks or something.
so, after two months of anxiously turning around
during the twenty minute drive to the store
feeling both defeat and relief,

> - my tighter skirts and dresses will gather dust in the closet
> - besides, it's winter and frumpy clothing will hide my bulge for now
> - tights look like long underwear on me anyway
> - something something i want ice cream

i have a complicated relationship with having a penis,
because i don't, but i do.
so here i am
standing in the women's underwear section,
nervously pacing, realizing i have no idea what size will fit,
and the #transfriendly target employee
who has been stocking underwear (stalking me)
for fifteen minutes while i sweat
coughs when i finally reach for tights,
in a way that lets me know "men" can't wear tights,
and that this #transfriendly does not approve of perverts

a gaff(e) is a lot of things.
it is a violent climbing, butchering, and fishing tool,
it is a not-very-nice word for an older person,
it is a fuck-up, and it is a laugh,
almost certainly at the person who fucked up.
a gaff is a thing people can wear if they want to hide the bulge in tights or jeans
or skirts or whatever
> that one can get from having a cock

and a gaff is to take a blow, take a hit, take the damage.
i knew this in the back of my head because trans person+google,
    and laughed in front of the employee despite my heart,
laughed because i knew i was about to steal underwear,
laughed because i knew i was a woman,
    not despite my dick but because of it,
but mostly, i laughed because i realized that if i laughed,
i'd be stealing a gaff while risking a gaff while gaffing at the gaff
    of the ersatz ally more synthetic than the tights in my back pocket

floating above your bones

we ate frozen blueberries out of a teacup
we were naked, in bed in our first apartment
you were laughing *really* hard and accidentally touched your hip,
leaving a violet trace on your body,
floating above your bones
with your perfect laughter lines

an elegy for the virginia possum i hit on state route 72

have you ever seen a mammal
maybe nine pounds small
head bowed beside the road
clutching its stomach
eyes shut
facing down
forehead to the pavement
waiting to die.

have you ever hoped
beyond hope
you could do anything
to make it faster—

painless—

make it undone
have you ever known to check its pouch for young
in case they survived

what of this is useful
i do not know
the bodies of knowledge and of prevention
and those of guilt and grief
have not been great about their promised correspondence
and no matter how devotedly i believe
that we meet again in the dirt
my faith is tested
at the soreness of your feet
at the gentleness of your grimace
at the incomprehensible and staggering pain of breathing through
on the side of a rainy december road
lit only by uncaring headlights
and hope for a quick turning of the world
inside out
about the axis
of what you felt it meant to be

working the register

i know you drive to work from 28 miles away
winding around those 6 arbitrary turns
that only exist because someone moved their fieldstones off-grid
to steal someone else's stolen land

i know you save $26 every other week with hope
despite the track record of your car's breakdowns,
that $115 wig is so pretty, truly

the trans woman you met at the club who said you weren't legit
until you spent some cash on quality tits and a downstairs job
can fuck right off

and despite what the woman-hating drag queens and cis gays of this world say
you're more legit than anyone's wallet,
and i'll lift that wig for you any day of the week

wintermoons

trot down the snowladen trail
before the sun spills their produce bag
nectarines
        tangerines
                clementines
                        blood oranges
rolling across last night's glass
unbroken but for the feet of mice
and everything left behind

two nuthatches cling
and hop downwards
(can you imagine hopping downwards?!)
encircling the trunk of a silver maple
fat slivers of the moon,
dancing down to earth
to flit up and meet again
among the canopy of the whole world

to do it again
thru and thru

GRATITUDE

—

    This book could not have been collected without the winter sunsets and the summer birds collecting me. I have so much gratitude for so many people who believe in me enough for this to exist. Mom and Dad, thanks for encouraging me to leave boy scouts to go hear poetry in the coffee shop across the street. Don, you helped me write my first poem, and Bill, you keep reminding me to write the birds. Heather, you rekindled an understanding in me that poetry was a world, and Gabrielle, that it is this one. Maryann, you made me understand that sharing my poems in this way was possible. Terra, you not only picked up this collection and gave it a chance, you've made a wonderful home for so many artists and writers. Everyone in and out of whitehall and the farmhouse, everyone who listened, thank you. Tom, what can I say. I am the luckiest sister on earth. Selena, I'll race you to every compost pile we ever make. Thanks for helping me turn this one over and over til it turned into something new.

ABOUT THE AUTHOR

—

Gabby Loomis-Amrhein is a trans farmer and naturalist who is particularly enamored of birds. She believes in liberation, love, pawpaws, riding her bicycle, and the collective power of people to overcome the conditions that keep us down. She carves spoons and gardens with her partner on a small farm in southern ohio. Featured in the Fall 2019 issue of the Recenter Press Poetry Journal, her poems can also be found in *Hoxie Gorge Review*, *Hematopoiesis Press*, and *Sheepshead Review*.

Gabby's work explores poetry, phenology, and historiographies of body and place. She hopes these poems will serve herself and others as the field guide she needed growing up, marking the passage of time between woodcock dance and trillium bloom, a record of having been, becoming, coming out.

Recenter Press is a Philadelphia-based publisher dedicated to sharing work that documents personal transformation, that speaks to the need for the revolutionary transformation of society, and captures our deep communion with the world.

Thank you for sharing this space with us.

—

re-centering:

to cut through deception and heal our alienation; to bring ourselves closer to Love, to Truth, and to Liberation.

—

More from Recenter Press:
Patrick Blagrave - *Profit | Prophet*
Doe Parker - *The Good House & The Bad House*
Terra Oliveira - *And Still To Sleep* and *An Old Blue Light*
Schuyler Peck - *To Hold Your Moss-Covered Heart*

Made in the USA
Middletown, DE
25 February 2022

61781375R00043